Noodle Words

Confucius inventing a hard language

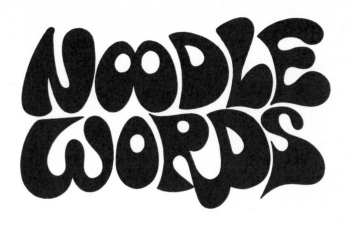

an introduction to Chinese and Japanese characters

by D. M. MURRAY & T. W. WONG

CHARLES E. TUTTLE COMPANY
Rutland, Vermont & Tokyo, Japan

Representatives

For the British Isles & Continental Europe:
SIMON & SCHUSTER INTERNATIONAL GROUP, *London*

For Australasia:
BOOKWISE INTERNATIONAL
1 Jeanes Street, Beverley, 5009, South Australia

Published by the Charles E. Tuttle Company, Inc.
of Rutland, Vermont & Tokyo, Japan
with editorial offices at
Suido 1-chome, 2-6, Bunkyo-ku, Tokyo

Copyright in Japan, 1971
by Charles E. Tuttle Co., Inc.

Library of Congress Catalog Card No. 79-147179
International Standard Book No. 0-8048-0948-8

First printing, 1971
Tenth printing, 1987

Printed in Japan

To ORVILLE and PAT,
who don't know Noodle
and to CHING-LING, who does

■ Table of Contents

■ Preface

To Westerners, Chinese writing looks odd. What is it—noodles? Doodles? Decorations for lampshades?

The fact is, Chinese people really say things with it. Things that an Ordinary Occidental would enjoy reading, like "Happy New Year" and "Fried Rice."

My co-author and I want to share this great discovery with other people. We have written this book for

> whoever visits Asian cities, or wants to,
>
> whoever goes to Chinatown for dinner,
>
> whoever wonders what it says on Mao buttons,
>
> whoever wonders what the Chinese villains are saying in the *Steve Canyon* strip.

We do not intend to give a course in written Chinese. We only want to explain a few common characters, and maybe dissipate some of the mystery about the language. And we would like to do this painlessly. Chinese without tears.

For those who may use this book as a springboard into deeper swamps of knowledge—and we think it is possible to do so—there are plenty of real courses and texts. In these days when the East is looming Large and Red, courses in Beginning Chinese are starting up all over the civilized Western World—and even in the uncivilized Western World, as in Alabama and Chicago.

For those who may become tourists in Asia, we would like to point out that a little learning in this area of the written language can be fun, can make you a more amiable ambassador of America, and can even save you money. You can warm the hearts of clerks, waiters, acquaintances, by reading a sign or writing a word. The Chinese know they've got a beastly hard, though very wonderful, language; and they're almost as proud of it as Frenchmen are of French. If you show a little intelligent curiosity, they'll make you an honorary member of the club, like you better, help you more, and maybe charge you less.

And what if you venture into the non-English parts of Asian communities? It's nice to know that the sign over the door means *bookstore* instead of *brothel*—or vice versa, depending on your tastes. Also, it's nice to be able to write a word for something you want to buy. In this way I once bought napkins and paper plates in a thoroughly non-English store, where the concept *picnic* was quite unknown. The whole staff (a family, of course) showed me how to improve my calligraphy, and the project became a major social occasion. In the end, everybody was smiling like mad, I had my napkins, and the price was slashed.

This is no lexicon for libraries, but in certain ways it is reliable. My collaborator is Chinese and a direct descendant of Confucius. So he knows the language. In fact, he won the well-known Hand-cramp Award (a silver Peking Duck) for being able to write the Chinese word *melancholy* three times in half an hour. Here it is:

I should add that we have taken a few liberties with history and etymology. Confucius didn't really invent the language, and the development of the characters was perhaps a little more complex than we have said: the word for *nine* may not have been a croquet wicket at all. We are neither of us Bernhard Karlgren, we're happy to say, and there are some things we don't know and don't even want to know.

But we have been accurate about how the modern characters look and what they mean. My co-author can be depended upon here. And we have been accurate about what the Ordinary Occidental *doesn't* know. I'm an O.O. myself and have contributed generously of my ignorance.

D. M. MURRAY

Hong Kong

■ Invention of Chinese Characters

In the beginning, Confucius said to his disciples, "Let's make up a real hard language. Everybody reads English, and what with jet travel and all, it's getting so most people even know some Italian and French—like *Sophia Loren* and *Brigitte Bardot*. Let's make up something real tough, so tough nobody but us can understand it."

"Great, OBoy–OBoy–OBoy," said the disciples.

Confucius was eating noodles at the time. He took his chopstick and flipped a few odds-and-ends of noodle on the ground. "See that?" he said. "We'll call that *laundry*." Then he stirred the noodles around a little with his toe. "That's *restaurant*.

洗衣店 **Laundry** 菜館 **Restaurant**

Pretty soon you'll see those words all over San Francisco."

"OBoy–OBoy," said the disciples.

After a while, though, the Chinese public began to complain. "Why can't we have a language we can *read*?" they said.

"What a bunch of dummies," Confucius thought. But he was really a kind man, so he went ahead and made some easy characters. This time he was eating fish, so he took one fishbone, sucked it clean, and held it out level.

"That's the number one," he said. Then he held out two bones, and then three. "Two, three."

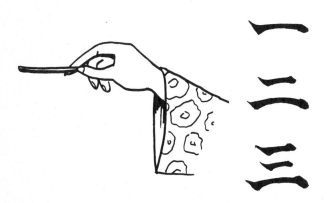

But they didn't seem very interesting to him, as characters go, and anyway he was running out of fishbones. Over on the athletic field, there were two kids hanging upside down from a parallel bar: what you noticed first was four bony legs in a square frame. "Hey," said Confucius, "you kids want to be the number four?"

"Neat," they said. "Write us down as four, Dad."

So Confucius drew a little picture, and then simplified it. "That's the number four."

Next he made an ordinary five out of uncooked noodles, and stood it up. The top piece had to be balanced, and the whole thing had to be reinforced with an extra noodle.

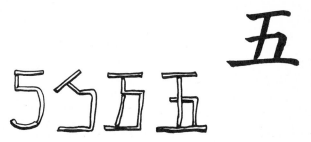

"That's a pretty dumb five," a disciple said. "Shut up," said Confucius. "Just learn it."

For six he drew a little picture of a coffee table with a vase on top. "That thing has six pieces," he said: "four legs, a top, and that little Ming porcelain." Then he simplified it.

Seven was a European 7 made out of wet noodle. The top fell and the middle part sagged. Several of his disciples started to comment, but Confucius said quickly, "Just learn it."

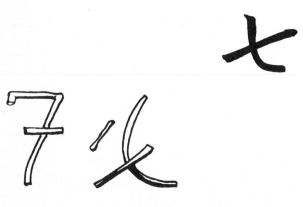

Eight and nine were croquet wickets, a little bunged-up by the feet of clumsy disciples:

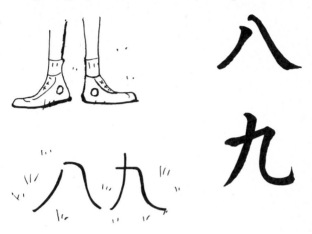

Ten was originally five short noodles laid across five long noodles, but it took too long to write that way, so he simplified it:

"That's our number system," Confucius said, "and if you don't like it, you can learn that illogical and unpictorial system the Arabs invented. Myself, I like the noodle-and-wicket system, even if it is a little too simple. And I think it will catch on."

"We're with *you*, Poppa Kung," said the disciples. So here they are:

一 二 三 四 五 六 七 八 九 十

十一 十二 十三 十四 十五 十六 十七 十八

十九 二十 二十一 二十二 二十三 二十四

二十五 二十六 二十七 二十八 二十九 三十

一百 一千 一萬

■ Meanwhile, Over in Japan

People were speaking Japanese.

This was a very fancy language, full of case endings and verb endings. Almost as bad as English. According to the philologists, Japanese belongs to the Finno-Ugrian group of languages. And as everybody knows, you get a bunch of Finnos and Ugrians together and they put out a terrific sound, full of variations. But it doesn't have any written words.

So when the Japanese wanted to read, they had to sail across the Sea of Japan for their books. The nearest Chinese province was called Go. "Go on over to Go, Joe," said the Emperor Kammu, "and get us some Buddhist bibles."

Reading led to writing, and of course they wrote in Chinese characters. The noodle-words didn't exactly fit what they were speaking, since Japanese had all those inflections and Chinese didn't. So the Japanese scholars made adaptations. Sometimes they used a Chinese character for its meaning, like Chinese 人 *jen*, which became Japanese 人 *hito*. And sometimes they used a Chinese character for its sound, like Chinese 日 (pronounced "rih") together with the Chinese 本 (pronounced "pan"); spoken as one word they sounded like the word *Nippon*, the name of their country.

One whole boatload of words from China got lost in a typhoon, and all the *L*'s sank.

The written Japanese language that finally resulted was pretty confusing to ordinary people, just like the first noodle-words were in China. So a smart man named Kobo Daishi invented a syllable-alphabet, to represent sounds with.

"An alphabet," said Kobo, "is a neat little idea I picked up from the Romans. Might as well borrow it—after all, the people of Rome get their motorcycles from us. We'll call our alphabet *hiragana*."

Now they had a language made of Chinese noodle-words and Japanese syllable-sounds, all on the same page. It was a real dish of sukiyaki. At this point, a lot of people simply gave up and went to Los Angeles to learn English.

But quite a few stayed in Japan too—as you can see when you try to cross a street in Tokyo—and these people went on using the Chinese characters along with the syllable-words.

So if you can read some Chinese characters, you can read a lot of street signs in Japan, like this one. It means "foreign goods store," and it's all Chinese.

Foreign

Goods
(three tin cans on a shelf?)

Store

As you see, Kobo Daishi's girlfriend has already figured out how to spell *saké* with *hiragana*.

Kobo Daishi inventing the *hiragana* syllabary

■ Pictures of People and Things

If you know some Chinese characters, then you know some Japanese.

And the way to learn the Chinese characters is to take a serious historical approach to the problem. Just think of Confucius, sitting there in a meadow in the Land of Lu, drawing things. First he did the numbers, then *woman* and *child* and *man* and *wine*—very basic stuff. Then the landscape—mountains and trees and animals and people. Once in a while somebody driving down the highway would stop and look.

"Whatcha doin, Poppa Kung?"

"Oh, nothing. Just making a language for you people and the Japanese to write with."

"Oh. I thought maybe it was something important. See you!"

Not that Confucius didn't enjoy his work. When he did *woman*, he sketched a young peasant dolly —she was carrying baskets slung from a shoulder-pole. They exchanged a few words.

"Nice pair of baskets you've got there, Hon!"

"Tee-hee!"

Confucius made a sketch chatting in a friendly way as he worked—about the weather and where she lived and what her telephone number was. He drew the bust-line carefully, then simplified the whole picture into a character.

女

Woman

"I may be an old man" said Confucius, "but I still get the point of things."

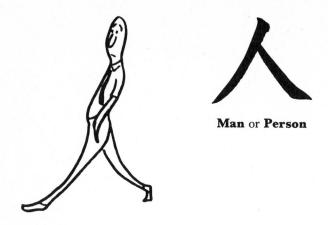

Man or **Person**

The man he drew happened to be walking—his wife had the car.

Child or **Son**

The child he drew was wearing a jockey cap at the time.

Confucius took a drink of rice wine then, to relieve his sense of sympathetic fatigue. After that he drew the wine. In the simplified character for *wine*, he added some drips alongside the bottle, to give a liquidy feeling to it.

Saké or **Wine**

Mountain

Sun

"It came out a little square," said Confucius, "but what the hell."

Moon

So he made the moon square too: "Moonlight is for squares anyway."

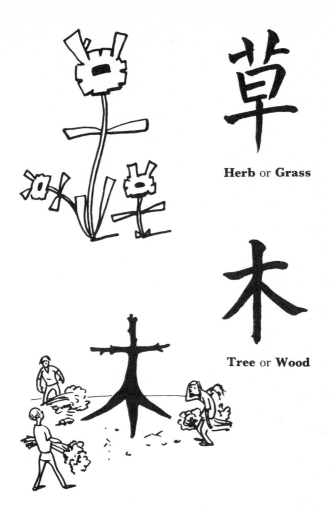

Herb or **Grass**

Tree or **Wood**

The tree originally had leaves, but Confucius had his disciples pull them all off so it would be easier to draw.

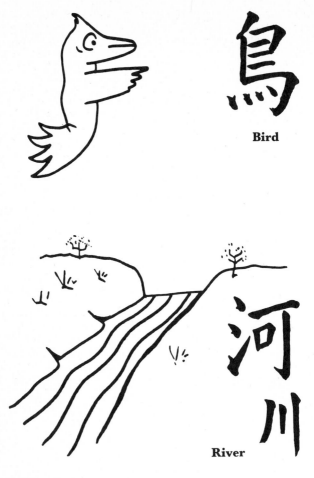

Bird

River

The little character on the bottom shows what he started with (stream, brook). The big one at the top doesn't look much like a river, but it has those drips that mean liquid.

Toad

Tortoise

It was hard to get the tortoise to stand on his tail like this. Confucius had to sing the Chinese national anthem while he drew.

Field

Feather

What this Indian was doing in a Chinese rice field, nobody knows.

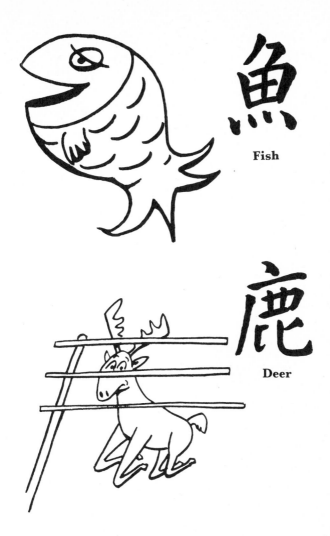

魚

Fish

鹿

Deer

The deer he drew was caught in a television antenna.

Pig

It was a very tired pig, taking it easy against the barnyard fence.

Cart or **Vehicle**

Confucius was looking at it from behind, as you can see. While he was drawing it, there was an accident. The cart got turned over on its wheel.

Hair

For this one, Confucius sketched a lady in a straw hat who was driving by. Her hair was blowing all over the place, but she didn't seem to care.

Roast

Word and **Mouth**

Ear

禾

Rice (growing)

米

Rice (hulled)

Rat

It was a gentle sort of rat, who posed gladly.
This was before rats got a bad name.

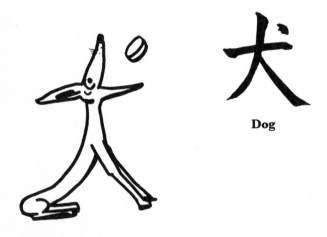

Dog

It was a thin dog, catching a biscuit.

Door or **Gate**

"It's not much of a door," Confucius said, "when you think how easy it would be to stoop under and go in without opening it. But that's the way they make them in Lu."

Landscape in Lu

After Confucius had done the whole landscape, he put the characters together and called it Landscape in Lu. Then he tacked it on a fence so people could learn the Chinese language.

As the 日

set behind the 山

Confucius picked up his

and walked off to the village

to look for the 女

*   *   *

The next day, Confucius made some idea words. "We've got to have some abstractions in this language," he said. "I can do it by putting together pictures of *things*."

■ Idea Words

Flight

For this, he sketched two humming birds flying through a bed of asparagus.

Bright

"Sun and moon together make 'bright'—people will think this is a real cute idea."

Good (woman and child together)

"I don't approve of women leaving their kids in nursery school," he said.

For the next one, he consulted his disciples. "We need a word for *much*, kids. What comes into your minds?"

"Money, lots of dough!" they said. "Two fifty-dollar bills!"

Much (two fifty-dollar bills)

■ Miscellaneous Characters

After he had finished the idea words, Confucius went ahead and made a lot of miscellaneous characters—about 40,000 of them. He didn't explain these—just said to the public, "O.K. now, learn 'em!"

As the Chinese people discovered, it wasn't easy. One thing that helped, though, was that Confucius had left clues in a lot of them. Part of the character gave a clue to the meaning. For instance, take the words that have something to do with *fire* or *water* or *wood*. Here are the *fire*, *water*, and *wood* clues:

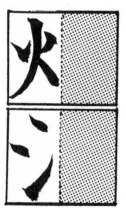 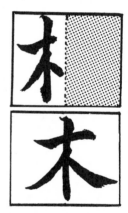

A person can pick out these clue-parts and make a reasonable guess about the meaning of the whole thing. Of course it helps if the word is found in revealing surroundings (words stamped on a fire extinguisher are likely to mean "fire extinguisher") or if you have a little assistance from a knowledgeable friend (like a Chinese instructor from Berlitz). But even without help, you can make good guesses. Here are some *fire-wood-*and-*water* words:

Fire Extinguisher

There's that drippy *water* in the top character, there's *fire* in the middle, and there are four *mouths* (yelling "Fire!") at the bottom.

火 險

Fire Insurance

Confucius obviously had in mind a small schoolhouse (with a flagpole in the yard) that was badly in need of fire insurance.

煙

Smoke

There's *fire*, and if you push the little handle at the right, a dynamite charge ignites, and everything goes up in smoke.

香 煙

Cigarette

The character at the left means "fragrant," like the first character of Hong Kong, "Fragrant Harbor." So a cigarette is "fragrant smoke." "Actually cigarette smoke and the Harbor both smell pretty foul," Confucius admitted, "but these euphemisms are good for business."

火 柴

Match

There's *fire* again, and at the right you can see the little *wood (tree)* element. It is a bit splintered at the top—the artist chewed on it.

Oven

The oven has two doors, and handles to turn on the gas with.

Forest

Trees all over the place.

浴室

Bathroom

There's the water, dripping down at the left. The mouth represents a chap singing in the bathtub.

淋浴

Shower Bath

This is not the most common term for it. Possibly this is one of those showers you find in national parks—in a little grove of trees near the privy.

■ Signboards in the Cities

Some years after he had invented the language, Confucius was talking to a bunch of tourists at the Mandarin in Hong Kong. "If you really want to learn Chinese," he said, "look at the shop signs. When I forget what words mean, I always come to Hong Kong and ride on the top floor of a doubledecker bus down Nathan Road. Up there at sign-level, you can read them easy, and the same words keep coming at you, again and again."

"You can go sign-reading in Taipei or Tokyo or Singapore or the Chinese parts of San Francisco or Toronto or Chicago just as well," he said. "I just happen to like Hong Kong, and the fare is only ten cents."

"What you see mostly on Nathan Road are signs for restaurants, banks, tailors, beauty shops, medicine shops, wine merchants, and ballrooms. Even if you can't read the whole thing, you can pick out the recurrent characters. For instance, a couple that turn up very often at the end of the signs are *company* and *association*:

公 司

Company

Association

"And you can recognize key characters like the one for *electricity*, which shows up in signs for electrical goods and telephone booths; and the one for *sea* in the signs advertising seafood or sea products, and the one pronounced *mei*, which is the first part of the word for *American* and also the word for *beauty* in *beauty shop*.

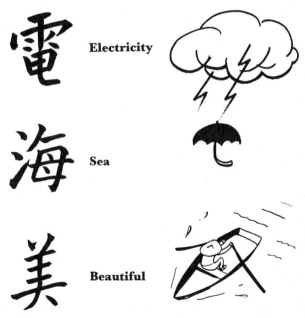

Electricity

Sea

Beautiful

Seafood

The last two characters on the right mean
Medicine Shop

"Remember that the beginning of a sign is usually the firm's name, like Hang On Handbag Company (owned by Joe Hang On) and that the signs read from top to bottom and from right to left. Of course wherever English has corrupted the language, as in Hong Kong, the signs sometimes read from left to right."

"Don't forget to look at the stuff they're selling, and don't forget to sniff the air. Why, on a hot day I can read the sign Sea Products on a shop in Queen's Road West from two miles away."

After he had told the tourists how to play Sign-Watching, he gathered his disciples together.

"Let's organize this game a little bit," he said, so as to make it easier for the tourists to play. Otherwise they'll switch to a game like Mah Jongg, and God knows we've got enough noise around here already. Suppose you're visiting an Asian city for the first time, disciples. What's the first thing you want?"

"A bank," said the disciples. "Yeh. Money-moneymoney!"

"All *right*," said Confucius. "Don't get carried away. Here's a sign for *bank*. As a matter of fact, it's the First National City Bank, on Queen's Road Central. You read from left to right and you end up with two characters that just mean *bank*.

The First National City Bank, Queen's Road Central, in Hong Kong. The last two characters on the right mean bank.

"Then what," Confucius asked. "You've been to the bank. What do you want after you're loaded?"

"Restaurants and Peking Duck," said the disciples. "Bar, Suzie Wongs, ballroom, hotel!"

"We'll just skip that Suzie Wong stuff," said Confucius, "but here are the others."

Moon Palace Restaurant
(San Diego)

Restaurant

Restaurant (another word for it)

Tien Heung Lau Restaurant
(Woo Sung St., Kowloon)

TWO RESTAURANTS
THAT HAVE ENGLISH SIGNS

In Hongkong

In New York

Peking Duck

Bar

Ballroom

"Do you think you'll be able to satisfy all your little animal-appetites now?" Confucius asked. "What about the next morning, then? I think you'll need *medicine shop, aspirin, barbershop, European type restaurant, breakfast, ham-and-eggs, post office* (to send for more money), *beach, swimming, Coca-Cola, seafood restaurant, movies,* and *nightclub.* That will start you off right, and give you another nice day."

"Of course," he added, "sometimes there's more than one term for these things—it depends on which part of the noodle-speaking world you're in. So I'll give you two terms when it seems advisable."

葯行　葯店 ············· **Medicine Shop**

阿司匹灵 ················· **Aspirin**

理髮廳　理髮店 ······· **Barbershop**

西餐廳 ····················· **Restaurant**
(European)

早餐　早點 ·············· **Breakfast**

火腿蛋 ····················· **Ham-and-Eggs**

—59—

郵政局　郵局	· · · · · · · · · · · ·	**Post Office**
海灘　海邊	· · · · · · · · · · · ·	**Beach**
游泳　游水	· · · · · · · · · · · ·	**Swimming**
可口可樂	· · · · · · · · · · · · · · · ·	**Coca Cola**

海鮮飯店
Seafood Restaurant

電影
Movies

夜總會
Nightclub

The disciples studied all these words with real enthusiasm. "A great list," they said. "A great language you've got here."

"I think this is turning into a guidebook for wild young bucks," said Confucius. "Now, for a change, let's take the ladies shopping. Fit them out, from their tops to their bottoms—I mean head to toe. Here are the words: taxi, bank, jewelry, ladies' tailor, cheongsam, hairdresser, cosmetics, handbags, stockings, shoes.''

的士　計程車 ····· **Taxi**

銀行 ····················· **Bank**

珠寶店 ················· **Jewelry**

洋裁 ··················· **Tailor** (Ladies')

長衫　祺袍 ········ **Cheongsam**

美髮師 ················ **Hairdresser** (Ladies')

化粧品　化妝品 ·· **Cosmetics**

手袋 ·· **Handbag**

絲襪 ·· **Stockings**

女鞋 ·· **Shoes**

"All right," said Confucius, "that ought to get them all dollied up. Now let's send them around to buy a lot of junk to send home. Otherwise they won't get all their husbands' money spent. Here's what they'll want: curios, camphorwood chests, brass, wicker, Thai silk."

古 董 ············· **Curios**

樟 木 箱 ············· **Camphorwood Chests**

銅 器 ············· **Brassware**

籐 器 ············· **Wickerware**

泰 絲 ············· **Thai Silk**

"Wow," said the disciples. "Better tell them the word for bank again, after all that."

"Shut up," said Confucius. "Now let's take them around a little. Show them the town. Tour, travel agency, guide, boatride."

觀光　遊覽 ·············· **Tour**

旅行社 ····················· **Travel Agency**

導遊 ························· **Guide**

遊船河　遊河 ·········· **Boatride**

"Send them home," said the disciples. "Let's talk about the word for Suzie Wong!"

"O.K., we'll send them home," said Confucius. "Airport, ticket, steamship line, baggage, passport, U.S.A."

飛機場　機場 ········· **Airport**

票　機票 ················ **Ticket**

輪船公司 ················ **Steamship Line**

行李 ························ **Baggage**

護照 ························ **Passport**

美國 ························ **U.S.A.**

"Suzie Wong," said the disciples. "Bar."
"The lesson's over," said Confucius.

■ Words to Eat with

The next time Confucius caught up with the tourists, he talked about menus. "Chinese food is good," he said, "but it tastes even better if you know some words for it."

"When you go to a Chinese restaurant, *show off*. Write 'pig meat' on a napkin and show it to the waiter. Here are the characters:

"Oh, pork! You write Chinese very well, Sir!"

"You can tip the waiter beforehand so he'll be sure to respond with the happy cry, 'Oh, pork! You write Chinese very well, Sir!' It doesn't matter if you don't happen to like pork. You will have impressed the hell out of your friends."

"Then, even if the menu has English translations, pick out some characters you can recognize:

Rice   **Chicken**   **Vegetable**

Noodle   **Shrimp**

"After you get to be good at this, go to a non-tourist place, which is about ten times cheaper and where the menu is all in Chinese, chalked up on a blackboard maybe. It will be a pretty wiggly script—it's called cursive style, and you can see why. But if you've had the foresight to steal a menu from the other place, maybe you can make out a character or two. Cursive pork looks like this:

"Here are some specific dishes to order by character: Chicken and fried rice (whether you like fried rice or not, Chinese restaurant people expect Americans to like it, so humor them), and

Chicken and Fried Rice

chicken and noodles (or, as they put it, "chicken and noodle"—they don't bother with our unnecessary English plural)."

Chicken and Noodle

"The john in these places, by the way, might be labeled with the characters below. But if you're really in Asia, you may not adore the place. At least don't expect wall-to-wall carpeting and rose-upholstered toilet seat covers."

Lavatory

■ Art:
The Oriental Wing in the Gallery

"The first thing to do in the Oriental wing of the art gallery," Confucius said, "is get yourself Oriented. If the goddesses have more than fifteen arms, you're in the Indian part. Move on. You'll recognize the Japanese section by the plum blossoms.

"In the Chinese section, there is stuff from five periods (though I may have forgotten a few). Here are the words:

商　　Shang　(1766–1122 B.C.)

周　　Chou　(1122–255 B.C.)

唐　　T'ang　(A.D. 620–907)

宋　　Sung　(A.D. 960–1127)

明　　Ming　(A.D. 1368–1644)

"**Shang** is funny looking things on legs, often considered attractive.

"**Chou** is junk—old pots that should have been thrown out long ago, and probably were.

"**T'ang** is pottery horses with fat little bottoms and necks. They came out of tombs 1,000 years old and they look as if they're going to prance off right now to the plains of Wyoming. This horse-pottery has a real tang to it.

"**Sung** is paintings. All the painters studied William Wordsworth and got a little nutty about Nature. So you see a shaggy mountain, big as creation, and a little guy in a pointed hat carrying sticks up a path. Actually, this is pretty realistic— you'll see, when you visit Victoria Peak in Hong Kong or the gorges of Nikko. The clouds are made of coiled macaroni, which shows the Italian influence.

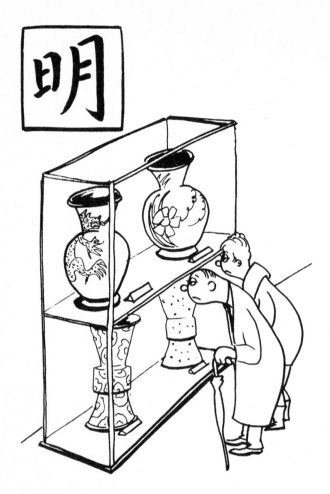

"**Ming** is vases. Very dull. The word *ming* means not only the dynasty, you'll remember, but also *bright*—sun and moon together. This is the only charming thing about the whole epoch. Forget it.

"Both Chinese and Japanese paintings have writing on them, as a part of the pictures. That stuff dangling in the seascape is not seaweed. It's calligraphy. Don't try to read it; it's illegible even to Chinese people. Maybe it's a poem, or maybe it just says 'Roll tightly before mailing.' It doesn't matter. Just admire it, because it *is* beautiful.

"The most important written words in the Oriental wing of the art gallery are these:

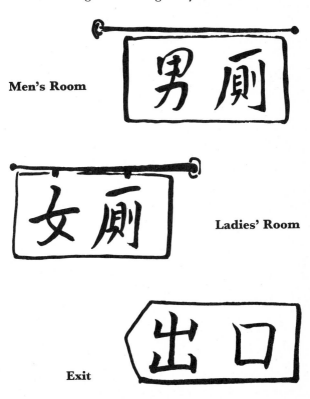

Men's Room 男厕

女厕 **Ladies' Room**

出 口 **Exit**

■ Some Signs That Give Warning

請勿吐痰

Please Do Not Spit

提防小手

Beware of Pickpockets

危險

Danger

Wet Paint

Please Don't Talk to the Driver

*　　*　　*

SOME SIGNS WE COULDN'T FIND ANY
CHINESE FOR:

John Loves Mary

Prepare to Meet Thy God

What—Me Worry?

Slogans of the American Century

Down with the American Imperialists

The East Is Red

Back to the Mainland

The Hong Kong British Must Definitely Come to a Bad End

■ Words You Already Know

CHINESE THAT BECAME ENGLISH

叩頭　　　**Kowtow**

長衫　　　**Cheongsam**

颱風　　　**Typhoon**

茶　　　　煙　　　　堂

Tea　　　**Yen**　　　**Tong**

ENGLISH THAT BECAME CHINESE

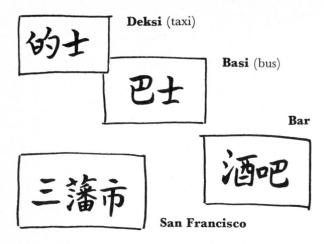

Deksi (taxi)

的士

Basi (bus)

巴士

Bar

酒吧

三藩市

San Francisco

JAPANESE THAT BECAME ENGLISH

腹切り	**Hara kiri**
空手	**Karate**
柔術	**Jujitsu**
廣島	**Hiroshima**

ENGLISH ON THE GINZA

Biya gaden	ビヤ・ガーデン
Hambaga	ハンバーガー
Appuru pai	アップル・パイ
Sutorippu sho	ストリップ・ショー
On za rokkusu	オン・ザ・ロックス
Shoppingu senta	ショッピング・センター

■ A List of Common Radicals

To make the acquaintance of Confucius seems to be the main initiation rite for most Westerners into Chinese culture. People hear about the sage, and take him to be representative of the essence of it. With this in mind, Mr. Murray, my co-author, has created for the West the legend that Confucius invented the Chinese language—an idea which is totally a stroke of the American imagination.

It occurs to me that readers might like to know, in addition to our Confucian fable, the "original" legend about the creation of the language.

It is said that during the 26th century B.C., Ts'ang Chieh (倉頡), who was the president of a commission of learned men appointed by Huang Ti(黃帝), one of the legendary sovereigns of ancient China, invented the language after the shape of natural things. For example, having seen the footprints of birds and animals on the sands, he made the word爪, which means "claw." It is indicative: that is, its form indicates the meaning. The sun is ⊙ (日); the moon 🌙 (月). These are pictorial: that is, they are representative of objects.

Chinese characters are divided into six groups and are constructed on the basis of "radicals," about 242 altogether. I shall not give a detailed presentation of them. Instead, I have prepared a list of some 35 common radicals which fall mainly into the three groups: the pictorial, the indicative, and the suggestive (the construction of which suggests the meaning). I shall give brief explanations and examples.

1 ☉ the sun—it was said that in the primitive age, there was a black speck or a shadow in the sun; and people called it a three-legged raven; now 日 , pronounced as *jih*

CHARACTER EXAMPLES:

旦 the morning, the dawn—the sun just above the horizon, *tan*

早 also means morning—the sun just at the top of a young tree 十 ; used in daily speech, equivalent to "good morning," *tsao*

明 bright—the sun and the moon 月 , *ming*

晶 crystal; brilliant, shining—three suns, *ching*

晴 fine weather, clear sky—the sun in a blue 青 expanse, *ch'ing*

2 山 hill or mountain—representing peak and valleys; now 山 , pronounced as *shan*

CHARACTER EXAMPLES:

岩 a cliff, a precipice—mountain and rock 石 , *yen*

峭 precipitous; harsh, severe, *ch'iao*

峯 the peak of a mountain, *fêng*

嶺 a mountain range, *ling*

島 an island, *tao*

3 巛 water—representing ripples, or flowing movement, now 水 , also 氵 , pronounced as *shui*

CHARACTER EXAMPLES:

冰 ice—the ancient form of 冰 is 仌 , which represents the cracks on the surface of ice, hence means frozen water, *ping*

池 a pond, *ch'ih*

江 a large river, *chiang*

汗 perspiration, *han*

洗 to wash, *si*

4 火 fire—the middle part 人 represents the shape of a fire, the two side-strokes are the sparks, now 火 , also 灬 , pronounced as *huo*

CHARACTER EXAMPLES:

灶 a furnace, a stove—fire and earth, *tsao*

灰 ash, *hui*

烟 smoke, *yen*

照 to shine, to illuminate, *chao*

炒 to fry, *ch'ao*

5 土   earth— 二 represents the surface and the lower stratum of the earth, ｜ suggests the growth of plants, now 土, also 圡, pronounced as *t'u*

CHARACTER EXAMPLES:

坐   to sit—man 人 on the surface of earth, *tso*

地   ground, floor, *ti*

坡   a slope, *p'o*

埋   to bury, *mai*

基   a foundation, a base, *chi*

6 木   tree, wood—representing the trunk of a tree with branches and roots, now 木, also 朩, pronounced as *mu*

CHARACTER EXAMPLES:

林   a woods—two trees representing a small forest, hence 森林 means a forest, *lin*

枝   branch, *chih*

根   root, *kêng*

松   pine tree, *sung*

架   a frame, a stand; to support, *chia*

7 屮   grass—like little sprouts or growths, now 艸, also ⺾ (草), pronounced as *ts'ao*

CHARACTER EXAMPLES:

花 flower, blossom, *hua*

葉 leaf, *yeh*

芳 fragrant, *fang*

茶 tea, *ch'a*

菊 chrysanthemum, *ch'ü*

8 禾 growing grain— ⌐ represents the stalk with drooping ears of grain, ⌣ the leaves, ∧ the roots, now 禾 , also 禾 , pronounced as *ho*

CHARACTER EXAMPLES:

秋 autumn, the fall—grain and fire, harvest time, *ch'iu*

稅 taxes, revenue—people paid taxes with grains, *shui*

種 seed; to plant, *chung*

稻 rice growing in the field, *tao*

積 to store up, *chi*

9 竹 bamboo—the leaves of which droop, now 竹 , also ⺮ , pronounced as *chu*

CHARACTER EXAMPLES:

笛 a flute, *ti*

筍　the tender shoots of a bamboo, *sun*

笠　a bamboo hat, *li*

筏　a bamboo raft, *fa*

筆　a bamboo pen, thus the Chinese brush; writing instrument in general, *p'i*

10 田　field— ☐ represents an enclosure, ✛ the narrow paths between rice fields, now 田, pronounced as *t'ien*

CHARACTER EXAMPLES:

男　man—one who uses his strength 力 in the fields, *nan*

界　a boundary, *chieh*

留　to detain, to remain, to keep, *liu*

畜　domestic animals; to rear, *ch'u*

疆　a border, a frontier, *chiang*

11 雨　rain— ⼀ represents the sky, ｜ the ascendence of warm air, ⊓ the descending of cold air, and ⸬ are raindrops, now 雨, pronounced as *yü*

CHARACTER EXAMPLES:

雪　snow, *hsüeh*

雲　cloud, *yün*

雷　thunder, *lui*

電　lightning; electricity, *tien*

霧　fog, mist, *wu*

12 𠂆　a man, mankind—representing the arm and the shinbone, the former hanging down, enjoining with the latter, now 人 , also 亻, pronounced as *jên*

CHARACTER EXAMPLES:

休　to rest, to cease—a man leaning upon a tree, *hsiu*

仁　benevolence, selfless love, *jen*

仙　a fairy, an immortal, *hsien*

住　to live; to stop, *chu*

信　letter; to trust—man and his words, *hsien*

13 𡛔　woman—in a humble posture, making a bow, the feminine in general, now 女 , *nü*

CHARACTER EXAMPLES:

好　good—a girl, *hao*

妖　weird; bewitching, *yao*

妙　beautiful, excellent, wonderful; young, *miao*

妻　wife, *ch'i*

妓　a singing girl; a prostitute, *chi*

14 👁　eye—in its socket between the eyelids, now 目 , *mu*

—87—

CHARACTER EXAMPLES:

盲　blind—the eyes "die" 亡 , *mang*

看　to see, to look at, *k'an*

眉　the eyebrows, *mei*

睛　the pupil of the eye 眼 which is used in daily speech, *ching*

睡　to sleep—the eyes "droop" 垂 , *shui*

15 凵 mouth—representing the lips—an opening, now 口 , *k'ou*

CHARACTER EXAMPLES:

吐　to spit; to vomit—mouth and earth, *t'u*

吠　to bark—mouth and dog 犬 , *fei*

味　taste, flavor, *wei*

吻　to kiss, *wên*

哭　to weep, to cry, *k'u*

16 言 words; to speak—mouth and error 辛 , now 言 , *yen*

CHARACTER EXAMPLES:

記　to record, to remember, *chi*

評　to criticize, to comment on, *p'ing*

詩　poetry, *shih*

誠　sincere, honest, *ch'eng*

誓　an oath; to swear, *shih*

17 手 hand—representing the fingers and the wrist, now 手, also 扌, *shou*

CHARACTER EXAMPLES:

打 to strike, to hit, *ta*

扶 to support, to help, *fu*

拿 to bring, to take, *na*

捉 to catch, to seize, *cho*

採 to pick, to collect, *ts'ai*

18 心 heart—representing the heart chambers and the blood vessels, now 心, also 忄, *hsin*

CHARACTER EXAMPLES:

忘 to forget—to lose 亡 one's heart, *wang*

怒 anger, rage, *nu*

怕 to fear, *p'a*

恨 to hate, *hên*

悲 grieved, sad; to lament, *pei*

19 犬 dog—the upper part represents its head and ears, the lower are its feet, now 犬, also 犭, *chüan*

CHARACTER EXAMPLES:

狠 fierce, vicious, *hên*

狼 wolf; cruel, vindictive, *lang*

獅 lion, *shih*

獸 wild beasts, *shou*

獵 to hunt, *lieh*

20 馬 horse—representing its head, mane, feet and tail, now 馬, *ma*

CHARACTER EXAMPLES:

馳 to go quickly, *ch'ih*

馴 tame, *hsün*

駐 to station temporarily, *chu*

騎 to mount, to ride, *ch'i*

驚 to startle; frightened, *ching*

21 鳥 bird—representing its beak, head, eyes, wings and claws, now 鳥, *niao*

CHARACTER EXAMPLES:

鳴 to sound; the cry of a bird, *ming*

鴉 crow, raven, *ya*

鴨 duck, *ya*

鴿 dove, pigeon, *ko*

鷄 chicken; fowls generally. Sometimes it is written as 雞, *chi*

22 魚 fish—representing its mouth, fins, scales, etc., now 魚, *yü*

CHARACTER EXAMPLES:

鮮 fresh, *hsien*

鯊 shark, *sha*

鯨　whale, *ch'ing*

鱗　the scales of a fish, *lin*

鱷　crocodile, *ngo*

23 🐍　worms, insects—originally it refers to a snake, coiling; now 虫, *ch'ung*

CHARACTER EXAMPLES:

蚊　mosquito, gnat, *wên*

蛇　snake, *shê*

蛋　egg, *tan*

蜜　honey, sweet, *mi*

蝕　to eat up slowly; an eclipse, *shih*

24 🥩　flesh, meat—representing a piece of chopped meat, now 肉, also 月, *ju*

CHARACTER EXAMPLES:

肥　fat; fertile, *fei*

育　to give birth to; to nourish, *yu*

肴　savory food; sacrificial meats, *hsiao*

胃　the stomach, *wei*

腦　the brain, *nao*

25 👘　clothing—like a bonze's cassock with open neck and buttoning on the side, now 衣, also 衤, *i*

CHARACTER EXAMPLES:

衫　　a shirt, a robe, a gown, *shan*

褲　　trouser, *k'u*

被　　a coverlet, bedding, *pei*

裝　　to fill up, to load, *chuang*

補　　to repair, to patch, *pu*

26 糸　silk—like a strand of thin silk, now 糸, *szǔ*

CHARACTER EXAMPLES:

絲　　the common word for silk—two strands of thin silk put together, *szǔ*

紙　　paper, *chih*

細　　small, delicate, thin, minute, *hsi*

線　　thread, wire, *hsien*

紡　　to spin, to reel, *fang*

27 皀　food; to eat— 皀 means the rich flavor of grains, now 食, also 飠, *shih*

CHARACTER EXAMPLES:

飯　　cooked rice, *fan*

飱　　meal; to eat, *sun*

餅　　biscuits, cakes, *ping*

飽　　to eat to the full; satisfied, *pao*

餓　　hungry, starved, *ngo*

28 肌   disease—representing a man leaning on something, now 疒, *ni*

CHARACTER EXAMPLES:

病   sickness; to be ill, *ping*

疲   tired, exhausted, *p'i*

痛   painful, *t'ung*

瘋   insanity; leprosy, *feng*

瘦   lean, thin, *shou*

29 介   roof—representing a walled house, now 宀, *mien*

CHARACTER EXAMPLES:

安   quiet, peaceful; to soothe, to settle—woman under the roof, *an*

守   to guard, to keep, *shou*

官   an official, *kuan*

客   a guest, a visitor, *k'ê*

宝   precious; jewel, *pao*

30 刃   knife—handle and cutting edge, now 刀, also 刂, *tao*

CHARACTER EXAMPLES:

分   to divide; to distinguish, *fên*

切   to slice, to cut, *ch'ieh*

刧   to plunder, *chieh*

判　to cut into two; to judge; to decide, *p'an*

利　sharp; profit; advantage, *li*

31 ��車　cart, carriage—should be seen horizontally 冊 , on two sides are wheels, in the middle is the compartment, all joined by an axle, now 車 , *ch'ê*

CHARACTER EXAMPLES:

軌　a track, a path, an orbit, *kuei*

軍　military; an army, *chün*

載　to load, to carry, to convey, *tsai*

輪　a wheel, *lun*

輸　to transport, to introduce, *shu*

32 走　walking or hurrying— 止 represents the toes, 彳 means to step forward, now 辵 , also 辶 , *ch'o*

CHARACTER EXAMPLES:

追　to pursue, to chase after, *chui*

逃　to escape, to flee, *t'ao*

送　to send, to give to, to accompany, *sung*

逝　to pass away; to die, *shih*

過　to pass, to pass by, *kuo*

33 示　a divine being, an omen; to manifest, to exhibit— 二 is the ancient form of 上 ,

"above"; 川 refers to the sun, the moon, and the stars, now 示, also 礻, *shih*

CHARACTER EXAMPLES:

祝　　to bless, to pray to—god, mouth, man, *chu*

神　　a spirit, a god; divine, *shen*

祭　　to sacrifice— 夕 is meat, 又 is hand, *chi*

祥　　happiness, good omen, *hsiang*

禁　　to prohibit, to forbid, *chin*

34 金　gold; metals in general, now 金, *chin*

CHARACTER EXAMPLES:

釘　　nail, spike, *ting*

針　　needle, pin, *chên*

鉄　　iron; strong, firm, *t'ieh*

銀　　silver, *yin*

錢　　money, *ch'ien*

35 丰　gem, jade—three pieces of jade linked together, now 玉, also 王, *yü*

CHARACTER EXAMPLES:

玩　　to play, *huan*

玲　　tinkling of jade pendants, *ling*

珠　　pearl, bead, *chu*

理　　reason, principle, to manage, *li*

瑩　　the luster of gems, jades; bright, *ying*